Chasing Excellence

A ZOOM! Operational Excellence Title

Jake Harrell, LSSBB

Meridian Publishing
Grand Prairie, TX
"Making the world a better place through knowledge"

ISBN: 978-0-578-72777-6

Library of Congress Cataloguing-in-Publication Data
Harrell, Jake
        Excellence in Execution / by Jake Harrell
        p. cm.
ISBN: 978-0-578-72777-6 (alk. Paper)
    1.   Business. 2. Self-Help Methods. I. Title.

CONTENTS

FOREWORD

By Kevin Briggs

Regardless of your pursuit, *Chasing Excellence* will benefit you in your drive to be "the gold standard". Jake takes the abstract concepts of key elements of excellence and brings them to life in concrete examples that are easy to comprehend.

Throughout my professional life I have been privileged to have more than one career path. Having worked in everything from Public Education, coaching high school athletics, to the Logistics and Warehousing Industry, I have seen a variety of disciplines strive for excellence. Jake's easy, step-by-step approach to meeting the challenges that we face makes setting our path to excellence that much clearer and attainable.

Chasing Excellence reads like an offensive play book. I have known many coaches that take these same approaches to developing highly successful athletic teams. I have worked with teachers who have used some of the techniques described here to become highly qualified in their fields. As an Operations Manager at a regional distribution center, I incorporated many of these tactics into my work routine and saw an immediate impact on my effectiveness, outcomes, and team cohesion.

I highly recommend *Chasing Excellence* to anyone who strives to be the best they can be. Either as an individual or as a leader of a team, you will benefit from Jake's simple approach to a complex endeavor.

Kevin Briggs
Partner, TBH Logistics
Logistics professional

INTRODUCTION

Have you ever noticed how life seems to operate in circles? It is as if a cosmic rule requires a concept or phrase to present itself over and over in your life, until you reflect and digest the content. In the past 5 years or so, I have dedicated my free time trying to perfect my performance as a leader within a large organization. I have read many books, taken numerous personality and leadership tests, and over-analyzed some of my actions. I have kept journals logging my workday and made precise time saving alterations to maximize my effectiveness. And yet, for all that, it seems that these books, tests, and habits all dance around the edge of an idea that I want to share with you. This idea is simple. This idea is powerful. And this idea can change your life. This idea is that *you can achieve excellence in any arena, at any time, regardless of circumstances, by applying a few simple concepts.* I truly want to paint a picture for you of exactly how to iterate towards excellence, regardless of the issue at hand. My aim is to provide a concise methodology to resolve any problem in life, whether it be personal, professional, career related, or political. I believe you can use the tools in this book to solve literally ALL problems. While perfection itself may be an impossible goal, providing tools and resources to iterate towards excellence can get you pretty close.

I am a particular fan of a phrase my personal mentor and colleague John R. Thacker Jr. likes to say.

"How do we get more of the outcomes we want, and less of the ones we don't, for the least possible resources?"

While simple and powerful, iterating toward excellence is not *easy*. It isn't easy, because it will require you to change the way that you think about things. This is a book about self-growth.

Throughout this guide, you will notice I address industry problems and personal problems. I even explore a few entirely theoretical problems. This is intentional. The solutions I am about to share apply equally well regardless of situation and applying them to disparate contexts may help break down the walls we sometimes place between different parts of our life. We learn how to "5S" at work, but our bedroom is a mess. We learn how to have a long, happy relationship with our spouse, but don't know how to maintain that kind of balance with our colleagues. We have been taught a series of ideas in our lives to apply in different situations without learning the one idea that brings them all together. It is my goal to present you with that one idea, and in so doing, I hope to influence you to a path of excellence, success, and prosperity.

In addition to the preface above, I feel it pertinent to share my inspiration. You see, I have worked in a wide variety of organizations ranging from fast food, retail, manufacturing, hospitality, grocery, distribution, human resources, carpentry, waste management, and even one job at a *medieval renaissance fair.*

Despite this wide array of industries, all of them have had exactly one thing in common. At one point or another, a manager, owner, supervisor, or key stakeholder has uttered the phrase "We want to be the gold standard in X". This keeps recurring in my professional career, so I finally had to ask the question; *does anybody know what this means?* It is a great idea, a nice thought, however how do you get there? What are the prerequisites? When does it happen? And how do I know when I get there? I hope to provide an answer to that, unveiling resources that can be directly applied to any excellence barrier. To pierce beyond theory, I will provide several examples at the end of this guide, and how you can find your corresponding path to excellence. I am choosing the phraseology "excellence barrier" to apply a paradigm shift to problem solving. Instead of thinking "this is a barrier to X", I hope to reframe your approach to "how quickly can I become excellent in X?". The intent is to rewire the problem-solving parts of the brain, removes hubris, ego, and pride, and uses those dynamics to problem solve rather than get in the way. In this way, we can not only achieve excellence, but do so quickly. And that is my hope for you.

Section One – Reprogramming Yourself

In this section, we examine four tools that can help you to reprogram the way you think about barriers to excellence, and how you should approach them. In the introduction, I told you this journey toward excellence in execution would be difficult. That is because it requires you to think about the way that you think and take active steps to change your way of thinking, your way of acting, and ultimately, your way of life. As you proceed through this section, take time to reflect on how your current modes of thinking might different from what is presented. Take time to perform the chapter exercises and commit to changing your way of thinking. As you do so, you will begin to see broad new vistas of possibility open up to you. What were once stone walls and closed doors become nothing more than barriers to excellence – even simple ones – that you are now equipped to overcome.

Chapter 1

Everything Is Your Fault

Imagine the following scenario. You are starting your first day as a Payroll Manager for 1000 employees. You haven't been trained on the tools, processes, or procedures required to do your job, but you are responsible for payroll today and it is due. The pay cycle comes to a close, and 15 employees are furious that they have been paid the wrong amount. Consider two possible responses:

Response 1: *"This isn't my fault; I haven't been trained properly!"*

Response 2: *"This is my fault. Let us investigate what went wrong so I can improve going forward."*

What is the difference between these two responses? Do you remember when I said this wouldn't be easy, because it requires changing the way you think? The difference between Response 1 and Response 2 stems from a different way of thinking. In the first example, the person responding fundamentally conceives of the world from a place that psychologists call an "external locus of control."

What is the difference between these two responses? Do you remember when I said this wouldn't be easy, because it requires changing the way you think? The difference between Response 1 and Response 2 stems from a different way of thinking. In the first example, the person responding fundamentally conceives of the world from a place that psychologists call an "external locus of control." In this paradigm, a person's destiny is crafted by persons, forces, and events external to the individual and largely outside of his control. This way of thinking deflects fault and blame. The person coming from this perspective also fears that admitting fault could result in punishment – another negative outcome outside of his control.

The second response stems from a fundamentally different paradigm. Psychologists call this an "internal locus of control." This perspective believes that a person's destiny is largely shaped by the choices that individual makes. This perspective not only accepts fault, but immediately thinks about what could be done differently to get better results next time. This is very different from "falling on your sword", which only involves accepting fault. In fact, "falling on your sword" usually results from a paradigm that is fundamentally one of external locus of control. The powerful part of Response 2 is not accepting fault but asking what went wrong and what can be done better next time. However – and this is an important point – it is nearly impossible to ask that question without accepting responsibility first. That is just how humans are hard-wired[1].

These differences in thinking affect differences in response. And these differences in response affect different outcomes. In the next pay cycle, Response 1 has fifteen errored pay checks again, while Response 2 has seven. When the employees come up, concerned about being paid improperly, let's see how this conversation might continue.

Response 1: *"This isn't my fault; I haven't been trained properly!"*

Response 2: *"This is my fault. In reviewing last week's mistakes, I discovered an "errored pay report" that can help me identify employees that have not been payed correctly. I have implemented using this before submitting payroll, but it seems as though this is insufficient to get the outcomes we want."*

---

[1] Tavris, Carol. *Mistakes Were Made (But Not by Me).* Haughton Mifflin Harcourt, 2007.

—

In the third pay cycle, Response 1 still has 15 errored pay checks, while Response 2 has finally achieved zero errored payments for the week. Let's continue the conversation:

Response 1: *"This isn't my fault; I haven't been trained properly!"*

Response 2: *"I discovered through investigation that some employees have an incorrect pay routing code and corrected that. I've changed my routine to check for this type of error and use the errored pay report, and it looks like this has solved my problem. No further action is required here; excellence achieved."*

You see, by simply owning the excellence barrier, Perspective 2 iterated towards excellence. Owning fault isn't to be confused with taking blame, or to be extrapolated into responsibility for world hunger. It is simply an internal locus of control. What you personally feel you have control over, you often do. If you are in a position of leadership over others, this can be a fantastic litmus test to use with them as well. When you mention an excellence barrier to a person under your leadership, do they say "Yes! How can we resolve this?" Or do they say, "Well it's actually because (insert something outside of their control)." Step one to riding the excellence train is owning the journey! You are the conductor, the stoker, and the engineer. To practice this paradigm, simply pick an area of opportunity, and ask yourself "have I been owning this"? If you don't own, you can't plan steps to improve, and if you don't plan steps to improve, how can you expect to?

Having an internal locus of control allows us to accept fault. Accepting fault allows us to plan for improvement. And that leads us to our second idea for achieving excellence in execution, which we will explore in the next chapter.

Chapter One Recap

     Pursuing excellence requires change, and change requires *taking ownership*. Instead of focusing on external forces that prevent excellence, own it.

Chapter Exercises:

1. Think of an area in your life that you are responsible for and your outcomes are less than excellent. Write it down.

    _____

2. How have you been approaching this problem?
3. Do you have a reason that shifts blame to other people or forces, or do you accept that it is your fault?

4. Now think of one or two areas in your life that you are responsible for and are quite successful. Why do you think you are getting excellent outcomes?

Where the rubber meets the road

Every chapter in this book includes a *Chapter Recap* as well as *Chapter Exercises*. These exercises are designed to help you think through your own excellence journey.

5. What does mindset mean to you, and how has it affected your responsibilities in life?

6. Now how will you think differently about the area of opportunity in question 1?

_____

_____

_____

_____

_____

Chapter 2

PDCA then PDCA then PDCA

PDCA is a common term in "Lean" enterprises, but if you are not familiar with it, is stands for Plan, Do, Check, Adjust[2]. This simple acronym is the life blood of searching for the "gold standard." We saw this approach in our payroll example from Chapter One, but there is a reason we addressed locus of control paradigm first – if you are not approaching excellence from an internal locus of control, Plan, Do, Check, Adjust can never lead you toward excellence. PDCA is an intentional, scientific approach to solving problems, that looks for the reason behind a barrier to excellence, attempts to mitigate it, and then measures the outcome. This "think, apply, test, and study" method is the only real way to sustain any excellence. When you strip blind luck away, PDCA or a similar methodology is all that remains when it comes to iterating toward excellence. *Plan. Do. Check. Adjust.*

Consider the following scenario (and trust me, at 6 feet, 1 inch tall and 260 pounds, I am well qualified to share this one). Three people, Larry, Bob, and Joe are overweight. They decide it best to write their weight down on a whiteboard in the office hallway, where they will all see it whenever they pass by.

Larry - 225
Bob- 237
Joe- 255

---

[2] The "A" in PDCA is sometimes referred to as "act"; however, the author uses the word "adjust" more commonly in continuous improvement training, because it implies an ongoing habit rather than a one-time execution.

The three friends agree to write their new weight on the board every week. After a week of lifestyle change, they write their weights down.

Larry - 220
Bob- 232
Joe- 250

All three people lost 5 pounds! All three are proud of their accomplishment. All three were able to do so by making a *Plan*. This is the first step in the PDCA cycle and critical to resolving any excellence barrier. Now let us take a look at week two.

Larry - 225
Bob- 227
Joe- 245

This time around, Larry went back to his original weight, and both Bob and Joe lost another 5 pounds. Why did Larry move backwards? Well, in this example, Bob and Joe both maintained their lifestyle change, while Larry got tired of the sacrifice and discipline and failed to *Do* his plan. It should not come as a surprise to anyone, but in order to achieve something, you actually have to do it! This is why gathering in a conference room and discussing an area of opportunity never really solves anything; it is a satisfactory way to *Plan*, but it doesn't *Do*. The doing is what nets us the results. Now let's take a look at week three.

Bob- 229
Joe- 245

Larry has decided that he is no longer participating, so he stops recording his weight. Bob gained 4 pounds back, and Joe remained the same. Bob is annoyed that he gained weight and is adamant about discovering why he went backwards – he had a *Plan* and he continued to *Do*, but he didn't get the results he was looking for. He begins logging all of his food intake and exercise time – he is collecting data to explain the outcome. This is the *Check* step of PDCA. Checking always requires observation and often requires collecting data in order to make an informed decision. Let's take a look at week four.

Bob- 227
Joe- 242

Not much has changed since week three, but Bob has a week's worth of data to review. He discovers that he made some errors in his calorie calculations and that riding an exercise bike burns less calories than lifting weights. He *Adjusts* his approach based on his findings – this is the A in PDCA. PDCA is really a loop: plan for change, do the change, check the outcome, and adjust your actions based on your findings. Let us take a look at final week five.

Bob- 220
Joe- 240

Bob is down 7 pounds! He conducted the 4th and most critical piece of the cycle, *Adjust*! You see, checking on anything in and of itself won't generate change. You have to *Adjust* your actions based on your findings. Imagine you are baking a pie, and when you open the oven, you see that the pie is engulfed in flames. Now what if you simply shut the oven and let the pie continue to burn? The *Check* didn't accomplish anything! Only when you *Adjust* your plan based on the results of the check will net you the outcomes you seek. Please put the fire out. *Please.*

Keep in mind that PDCA is designed to be a recursive loop. It is not designed to provide a perfect solution now; it is meant to iterate towards a favorable outcome. If you plan an improvement and still don't like the outcome, do it again. And again, and again, and again. If you are satisfied with your results, welcome to excellence! This is an important point – individuals and organizations who fail to achieve excellence often make "best" the enemy of "better": a project, plan, tool, or methodology might not be approved until senior leadership is convinced it will be excellent.

That is a recipe to fail. Almost nothing is perfect right out of the box, and we all crawl before we walk and walk before we run. Don't throw out tools, processes, or even people and try to start fresh. Try PDCA first. Often this will result in an organic improvement that gets you sustainable results with less effort and cost.

In the weight challenge example above, we have a made-up character who decided the excellence barrier was his fault. He then utilized PDCA to iterate towards the results he wanted. Contrast this with the baker who left that poor pie on fire, exclaiming "This is not my fault; I wasn't trained properly!" Both of these examples are fairly simple and easy to understand, so in the next chapter, we will talk about an idea that can help you solve problems that are highly complex, or even entirely foreign to you.

Chapter Two Recap

Excellence is not the result of a single action. It requires assessing the current state, creating an improvement action, measuring the outcome of that action, then adjusting your approach and acting again. Excellence requires a cyclical approach.

Chapter Exercises:

1. Think of the four elements of PDCA. Can you think of a time you tried to solve a problem without doing the "Plan" step first? How did it work for you?

2. Have you ever tried to fix something and then failed to "Check" the outcomes? What happened after a couple of weeks?

3. When considering the "Adjust" step, what are some barriers you might encounter when trying to modify a new plan? How might you overcome them?

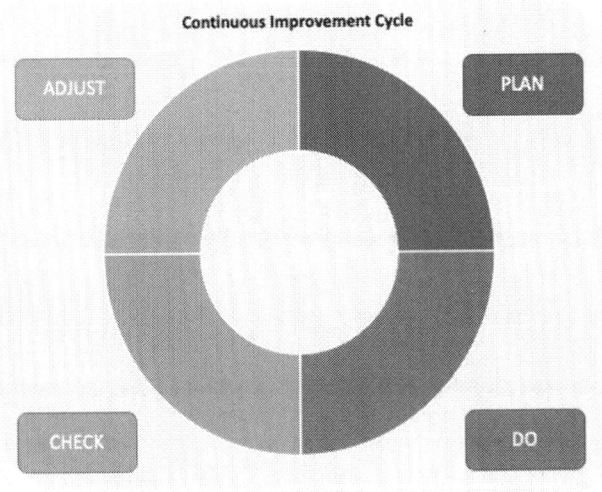

Continuous Improvement Cycle

Chapter 3

Breaking Down Complex Barriers

In the first two chapters we used some simple and familiar problems to illustrate how a person can use the internal locus of control and PDCA to iterate toward excellence. In this chapter we want to explore how you can still iterate toward excellence even in complex, unfamiliar, and extreme situations. To do that, we have a complex, unfamiliar, and extreme story for you!

In this scenario, long-time political figurehead Sara is chosen for an extremely weird new career. She is being nominated for president, but *on a different planet*. In this absurd example, planet Victon is seeking a human candidate for President, as the native inhabitants don't trust each other enough for one of them to mount a viable candidacy. In fact, this planet is inhabited by two distinct races of aliens. One race is the Giraffe People, and the other is the Crab People. The long necks of the Giraffe People make the Crab People feel insecure, and the Giraffe People look down on the lowly Crab People. Literally. The Planet Victon Political Consultancy Group has determined that a "medium necked candidate" would be ideal, so Sara is abducted from her bed in the middle of the night and spirited off to Planet Victon to run for President.

Sara takes some time to recover from her shock, but being a hard-charging political hawk, she quickly grasps the socio-economic struggle gripping the planet. However, as she asks questions and begins to learn about this strange new world, the Minister of Finance informs her dourly that the Super Apples are

22% below their traditional harvest rates, and an unexpected purple tide, which normally only happens once a decade, has led to too many lemons floating ashore. Gravity is changing daily and the moon is in retrograde. Victon is facing an endless list of serious problems. Sara now has quite a list of excellence barriers. She has no clue how to begin to approach the issues presented to her (*heck, neither do I, and I am writing this*). In fact, Sara doesn't even have a framework within which to make sense of these problems. Sara might be tempted to think she can't do the job, let alone achieve excellence, but Sara would be wrong.

Thankfully, Sara knows my secret. Sara knows that solving complex and unfamiliar barriers to excellence can be achieved by implementing two tools: breaking complex problems down into solvable chunks and listening to subject matter experts. Sara decides to solve the problem of getting elected first. To do this, Sara doesn't need *all* the information, just enough information to influence people's voting choices. She doesn't understand what it might be like to be a Giraffe Person nor a Crab Person, so she hires a political consultant who tells her that the Crab People are most concerned with the lemons washing ashore, as this raises the acidity of their natural habitat.

Without wasting time, Sara mounts a campaign to blame the lemons washing ashore on the Giraffe People. The Crab People, not being entirely aware of how propaganda works, assume a sense of solidarity with Sara and decide to give this "medium-necked candidate" a shot. Sara had zero knowledge of the situation, but she was able to iterate toward her goals by breaking the problem down into chunks and listening to a subject matter expert who *did* know about the situation. Now that Sara has the Crab People vote, she can move on to the next small, solvable chunk. She hires a Super Apple advocate and a Lemon liaison to consult on these respective issues. Based on the information they provide, she dives deeper into the "why", solving one micro-step at a time until she gets the outcomes she is looking for.

Sara breaks out her tasks into the following list:

- Hire an expert for "super apples" to discuss harvest rates.
- Hire an expert to consult on how tides and lemons are related.
- Hire an expert to consult on changes in gravity.
- Hire an expert to consult on the status of the moon.

Even though Sara's situation is overly complicated, and she has zero experience solving these complex problems, these bullet points all represent *achievable first steps*. The power of a simple bullet-pointed list is unparalleled. Sara is able to accomplish all six bullet points with relative ease. Notice how she broke her complex problem down into solvable steps and utilized subject matter experts to inform her on the facts of each point. Having taken these first two steps, Sara's next step for all points is the same:

- Gather data and make an informed decision

Sara discusses the problems and issues and *listens* to the subject matter experts. This allows her to work collaboratively on solutions that propose real change. At this point, Sara is able to move easily into the PDCA cycle we discussed in Chapter Two.

Sara can swiftly and effectively remove excellence barriers on an alien planet, with entirely made up circumstances by utilizing this skillset. I wonder how powerful this tool is on earth in mundane, regular old, day-to-day excellence barriers?

I apologize for the absurdity of this story, but it highlights the power of this tool: regardless of the complexity of an "excellence barrier", if you break it down into pieces that are simple enough to solve, you are in fact iterating towards excellence. When you rely on subject matter experts to inform you, you are iterating towards excellence. And when you use these two methods to inform your decision making, you can improve almost any situation, regardless of how foreign it may be to you. You see, Sara's journey doesn't *end* with breaking her problem into chunks and listening to subject matter experts, and it didn't begin there. It began with taking ownership of the opportunity (*Everything is Your Fault*). Sara's journey to excellence continued by breaking down her complex excellence barrier into solvable chunks. Sara was then able to *PDCA* a small chunk until she got the results she wanted.

This is the journey toward defining the gold standard. Where are we today? Where do we want to be? How do we define it and how do we get there? Follow this mindset and iterate towards the outcomes you are looking for. Remember, *chasing excellence* is primarily an issue of mindset.

The story of Sara is important because it reminds us that in the real world, we can rarely see all the potential actions to take, and certainly can't predict their outcomes. In this way, excellence barriers are very much like a game of chess. Chess has a defined set of rules and possible moves; however, 4 moves into a chess game there are 318,979,564,000 possible variants. You may find yourself in a sea of variations, asking yourself "this particular variant of an opportunity area has never been seen before; how can we possibly be prepared for this?" Well thankfully, we have a tool that prepares us for this – which we will look at in the next chapter.

Chapter Three Recap

Breaking down complex berries requires identifying small chunks of a problem that are individually solvable. Sometimes, these smaller chunks need to be broken down further until each step is manageable. Solicit and listen to subject matter experts to gain knowledge about topics that you are ignorant of.

Chapter Exercises:

1. Can you think of a time in your career when you had a problem so large or complex that you felt the barrier to excellence was insurmountable? How might you have solved it now that you know how to break complex barriers down?

2. Now that you know the pivotal role that subject matter experts play in making informed decisions, how are you thinking about personal relationship problems? Do you believe therapists and counsellors can add real value to your life? Do you think ego might get in the way of using subject matter experts like this?

3. List a complex barrier you are currently facing in your life. Break it down into chunks and list some subject matter experts you might use to help solve it.

*Excellence Barrier:*_____

_____

_____

Solvable Chunks	Subject Matter Experts

Chapter 4

Applying Theory in the Dark

This idea is one of the hardest concepts in this book to absorb and apply appropriately in life, but the outcome is worth the effort. This tool allows you to quickly iterate toward excellence on your own – even when you are faced with a lack of specific knowledge. This tool is especially helpful in moving the ball forward without specific input from your superiors.

Consider the following story:

Cody is married to an absolute germophobe. Cody arrives at home before his spouse and notice a mess on the kitchen table. Specifically, a bag of chips has spilled out all over the table. Cody knows his spouse is going to be upset, so he races to clean it up. Cody knows that his spouse is a germophobe, and that a food spill is a likely irritant, so he knows instinctually to clean it up.

Now what if we replaced the bag of chips with something else? Would the story change? Let us take a look.

Cody arrives at home before his spouse and notices a mess on the kitchen table. Specifically, a bag of flour has spilled all over the table. Now Cody knows his spouse is a germophobe, so he races to clean it up.

You are probably starting to piece together the concept here. You don't necessarily need to have *all* of the answers to *every* variant of an excellence barrier, you only need a solution to one that is *close enough* to apply successfully! Once applied, following the PDCA loop will quickly reveal how effective your solution is and how you can improve it. Now let's look at a problem with added complexity, where the issues seem unrelated, but correlated solutions can be applied.

Cody works for a distribution center as a supervisor. Recently, his new boss has had a series of meetings about improving employee accountability. Cody understands that as a business, his organization is too forgiving with policies that directly impact business success. The direction given is to conduct training for any first occurrence of policy violation, then give a written warning for the second violation. Cody is committed to this new direction when the following occurs under his supervision.

Employee James is found driving his forklift without wearing his seatbelt, which is a violation of site safety code. Cody observes this and after inspecting his training file verifies that James has had been trained to wear his seatbelt, and so Cody applies the appropriate accountability. The employee apologizes and corrects his error, and later on Cody gets a handshake from his boss for doing a good job with accountability. However, on the following day, James is doing something else.

Employee James is found with one leg tucked under the other one while operating his fork truck, using a single leg to operate both the gas and the brakes. There actually isn't a safety rule prohibiting this behavior, but it is clearly unsafe. What should Cody do? Should he just talk to James? Write him up? Fire him? Take no action? Well this is an excellent opportunity to use our fourth tool - *applying theory in the dark*.

Applying theory in the dark is the practice of understanding the values that underly your current situation and extrapolating them to the issue at hand. In this case, Cody should educate James that his behavior can affect his safety while operating a forklift. However, Cody doesn't stop there – he writes a policy describing this behavior as unsafe and presents it to his boss. Cody already knows the boss wants training and accountability, and Cody already knows that training does not exist for this opportunity variant. Cody doesn't need to ask permission to address the issue, and he certainly shouldn't fail to address the issue. As long as Cody can *apply theory in the dark*, he can take appropriate action immediately.

In fact, as long as you can discern the general direction of your leadership, your spouse, or your successful peers when it comes to an excellence barrier, you can generally *apply theory in the dark* to reach an appropriate solution. Since this concept has incredible value and takes quite a bit to master, let us review another scenario, visualizing this approach from a different angle.

You are hired into an advertising agency as the "Director of Operations". You are in charge of many duties, and responsible for driving excellence in an advertising environment. However, your boss makes it clear that fixing the turnover ratio within the agency is a top priority. A week into your new job, you learn that your company has an internal social media app that is being actively used to showcase newly earned business and the like. Do you see the how you can use this app by *applying theory in the dark*? You can use this app to praise employees and recognize them publicly, encouraging a reduction in turnover. This seems like a straight line, correct? You understood what your boss valued and were able to apply that knowledge to leverage a seemingly unrelated tool toward that end.

What if instead of turnover you were charged with increasing productivity by 5%? Or with promoting talent within the company? Or creating a new benefits plan? What if you were charged with reducing electricity usage by $2000 a month? All of these opportunity variants have similar solutions. If there is a tool in place that provides a solution, and that solution can be applied successfully, apply it! That is the practical application behind *applying theory in the dark*. You may not have the right screwdriver for the screw you need to remove, but if you have the "wrong" screwdriver and it fits reasonably well, results are results.

Congratulations! You have now learned the four core mindset changes that will allow you to achieve excellence. Be sure to do the section exercises, practice, and remember that this is about changing your mindset more than anything else. In the next section, we will to switch gears a little bit and discuss some ideas for fostering collaboration and relationships.

Chapter Four Recap

Applying theory in the dark is the habit of examining an excellence barrier and assessing whether your existing tools and directives can supply you with a means of resolving it.

Chapter Exercises:

1. Think of your current work responsibilities in terms of opportunity – name one opportunity that you could solve by applying theory in the dark.

2. Now think about your boss. Is she the kind of person that would appreciate you taking initiative by applying theory in the dark? Why do you think that is?

3. Can you think of a directive or mandate that your boss or company has tasked you with that you could apply to other areas of your work responsibilities?

$$N = R_* \times f_p \times \quad \times f_l \times f_i \times f_c \times L$$

Section Recap

Section one is about you – changing the way that you think. As you orient your thinking around the pursuit of excellence, your behaviours will follow. In the same way, as you change your behaviours and begin to implement the tactics found in this book, your thinking will change. It is a feedback loop.

Everything is Your Fault

The purpose of this section is not to make you feel guilty, but rather to help you take responsibility. Until you arrive at the point where you can accept responsibility for the outcomes you are experiencing, it will be very difficult for you to effect meaningful change. If you find this difficult, your ego might not be mature enough to support your pursuit of excellence. Spend time every day meditating on the power that you have over your own life and responsibilities. You have the power to overcome barriers to excellence and create change. And that means that if you aren't, it is your fault. Own it.

PDCA, then PDCA, then PDCA

This concept is designed to move your mode of thinking. While many people think of solving problems in terms of taking a one-time action, true excellence comes from a cycle of actions. This includes Plan – taking the time to study and understand the problem, Do – acting on your hypothesis, Check – studying the outcomes of your action, and Adjust – modifying your plan on the basis of your observed outcomes. This starts the cycle all over again. As you pursue excellence, consider that most barriers to excellence require an ongoing effort of cyclical thinking, rather than a "magic bullet" solution.

Solving Complex Barriers

There are two main takeaways from this section that are designed to reorient your thinking about problem solving. The first is that some problems have to be broken down into smaller pieces before they can be solved. The second is that other people can be an indispensable part of solving problems. You don't have to have all the answers on your own. Use your team to overcome these kinds of complex barriers to excellence.

Applying Theory in the Dark

This mindset change is designed to help you think of similarities between different barriers to excellence, and not shy away from solutions that are "good enough". Not every barrier to excellence needs a lengthy or rigorous analysis and solution. If you have some general guidelines or mandates, these directions can provide enough of an orientation to quickly overcome less complex barriers to excellence.

Section Two – Dealing with Others

In Section One we looked at four concepts fundamental to chasing excellence. This paradigm shift is a necessary prerequisite to the rest of this book; if you can't agree that *everything is your fault*, if you don't approach problems with *PDCA then PDCA then PDCA*, if you don't *break complex barriers down into solvable chunks*, and if you don't know how to *apply theory in the dark*, then you will have difficulty removing barriers to excellence and iterating toward the gold standard. However, all meaningful improvement involves teams of people working together. For this reason, you must master the three tools for dealing with others. One question that I receive frequently when coaching others is something like the following:

"What if I have found a good answer, but when shared with peers, friends, or team members, they claim it doesn't work?"

This is an unfortunately common experience. Perhaps you use some of the principles in this book to develop a valid solution proposition with your peers. Sometimes, the successful solution is labeled by at least one member of the team as "ineffectual or insufficient", sometimes without even giving it a try. When this happens, it can feel like a steel cage. How do you apply any theory or concept, if somebody is just going to say it won't work or they have already tried it and it doesn't work?

This resistance to change or accept another person's change proposal is, for better or for worse, a part of human nature. As you chase excellence, be cognizant of human psychology, and exercise prudence in your approach toward others. Involving others often and frequently in your excellence journey is a good way to build early buy in, which is a necessary prerequisite to chasing excellence in a team context.

In the following section, we will look at three tools that can help you gain the support and consensus of your team as you iterate toward excellence.

Chapter 5

Soliciting Feedback

When it comes to interacting with others to remove excellence barriers, there are few tools in your toolbox more powerful than soliciting feedback. Before releasing this book, I selected a peer, a direct report, and a personal friend to read it and provide me with feedback. In the workplace, before creating a change plan, solicit feedback from as many stakeholders as possible. This approach has two significant benefits. First, it allows you to learn – chances are that your team has better or at least more comprehensive ideas about excellence than you do on your own. Second, by involving others, you increase their buy-in and cooperation. This may sound easy, but you have to have a clear output in mind before getting started. It is easy to let ego get in the way and hinder your progress and results.

The reality of soliciting feedback is that it might not always be 100% positive. So prepare yourself mentally.

Let us take a look at an example, taken from my personal life. I will provide a modified story first, (one where ego gets in the way) and then the real story, where we utilize feedback to remove an excellence barrier.

Jake, entering professional development meeting: "Hey John, what is keeping me from growing my professional brand?"

John: "Do you want critical feedback?"

Jake: "Of course."

John: "If I am being transparent, I would like to recommend a book about executive presence. To start, your posture is poor at times, and you have a habit of excessively biting your nails. I am not saying these are deal breakers, but they do affect your professional image."

Jake, ego present and in the way: "Well, my posture is because I have had an administrative job for several years in the past. I can't control that I work at a desk all day. And my nail biting is nobody's business."

Do you see the challenge for ego driven Jake? He let ego get in the way which prevented him from addressing his excellence barrier. Jake has not yet accepted *everything is my fault.* The entire purpose of soliciting feedback was to improve Jake's professional brand. I received very good feedback that would go a long way to removing my excellence barrier, but I didn't use this information or make any progress. Let us take a look at this conversation again, and what happened differently in real life.

Jake, entering professional development meeting: "Hey John, what is keeping me from growing my professional brand?"

John: "Do you want critical feedback?"

Jake: "Of course."

John: "If I am being transparent, I would like to recommend a book about executive presence. To start, your posture is poor at times, and you have a habit of excessively biting your nails. I am not saying these are deal breakers, but they do affect your professional image."

Jake: "Thank you for the critical feedback. I have yet to receive feedback as actionable as this and it is truly appreciated."

John: "You are very welcome."

Do you see the difference in this conversation? I came in looking for an avenue to grow my professional brand at work and received some really good feedback. If we understand how to focus directly on getting feedback, we only need to ask ourselves "does this help remove the excellence barrier, or not?" Now in this particular example, the feedback given definitely helped remove the barrier. But what if the advice you get *doesn't* help remove the excellence barrier? I would like to suggest – you guessed it – a mindset change.

When soliciting feedback, consider *positive* feedback as *anything that can help you remove an excellence barrier.* This is a far cry from the popular perspective where positive feedback is often understood as feedback that makes a person feel good. On the other hand, consider *negative* feedback as any response which *does not reasonably address the excellence barrier.* This mindset change is essential, because it helps to orient your paradigm away from your personal feelings, which are subjective, and toward the excellence barrier, which is objective. For example, if you ask why your car blew up and what you can do about it in the future, your mechanic might reply, "Dumbass! You didn't change your oil in 15,000 miles. Of course you blew it up. That was really stupid – next time follow the manufacturer's recommended service interval." Well in the past, you might have considered this negative feedback, but, as grouchy as the reply sounds, it is actually positive: the mechanic gave you actionable feedback that you can use to get better outcomes next time! Conversely, imagine if the mechanic replied, "Oh, don't worry about it man. It wasn't your fault; better luck next time." This may sound empathetic to you, but it is actually negative – the mechanic has not provided you with actionable advice to address the excellence barrier.

So how do you handle these two types of feedback? The answer is simple.

When feedback is *positive* – take action!

In the example above, I received two pieces of advice: read a book on executive presence and improve my posture and nail biting. I purchased the book recommended to me and read it. I then set time on my calendar to stretch and try to slowly correct my posture daily. Also, I am proud to say I have given up biting my nails. This is a huge accomplishment for myself personally, as it is a habit I had held onto for 17 years (and boy do my nails look delicious as I type this).

When feedback is *negative* – take action…if reasonable!

The first question to ask yourself when given negative feedback is "even though this feedback doesn't help remove our excellence barrier, is it actionable anyways?" This is an important step. Thinking about negative feedback this way helps to take your ego out of the equation and can open doors to improvement that you might not have considered, even if the advice doesn't directly address the barrier to excellence that you are currently facing. In my professional career, I have received all kinds of feedback. I have received great, good, stupid, logically flawed, and even directly counter intuitive advice, sometimes even when I didn't ask for it.

At one point in my career I was a cashier for a large grocery chain. One of the job requirements was to keep a minimum of 60 units scanned per hour (UPH). This requirement was a key component in assessing annual raises, so it was important to me. Evaluations were coming soon and I found that if I really pushed myself, and signed out of my station when not in use, I could average 300 units per hour. To my consternation, I received a "poor" performance evaluation with the note "you need to improve to 60 units per hour or face progressive discipline." Physically printed on the evaluation was my current UPH for the year, which was just over 280 units per hour. I was not only the best in the building, but I was the best in the state! I immediately sought out my supervisor, and asked for feedback on how I could improve, but the only feedback I received was "everything isn't about the numbers". Well, when it comes to my annual raise it sure is, LINDA! (Let me take a moment to step back from my feelings). In this case, the feedback was entirely negative – it didn't provide me with anything I could take action on to remove my barrier to excellence. However, it was a good indicator that my boss and I weren't aligned on what constitutes good performance. This is an opportunity to engage in dialogue and find out why that gap exists, and perhaps what action you could take to close it.

If the negative feedback isn't actionable, just thank the person and move on. No harm no foul, and nothing further needed. However, keep in mind that most feedback that doesn't directly address your barrier to excellence is still actionable and might have benefit from being acted upon.

Imagine this fictional exchange between me and John:

Jake: "My diet is poor, and I am overweight; can you recommend a workout program for me?"

John: "If I am being transparent, I would like to recommend that you address your executive presence. To start, your posture is poor at times, and you have a habit of excessively biting your nails. I am not saying these are deal breakers, but they do affect your professional image."

John's reply does not address the excellence barrier I was seeking to remove and could actually come across as offensive. However, if the negative feedback doesn't hurt you and isn't counter-intuitive to your end goal, but it *is* actionable, take action anyway. Training yourself to do this will help you address all kinds of peripheral issues which can only help you, and grooms your approach to focus solely on outcomes, and not inputs. Let us take a look at how his feedback, although it doesn't impact our excellence barrier, can assist us if we still take action.

- We build a fantastic relationship with the people we solicit feedback from when we demonstrate that we take action according to their feedback.
- The person giving the feedback is twice as likely to give you honest, transparent feedback in the future should you require it.
- We build self-discipline around taking action when feedback is given, grooming us for better utilizing a positive feedback outcome in the future.
- Correcting the nail biting wouldn't affect me in any negative way, and in fact gives me a positive outlook on the entire interaction.
- I may not have realized my posture was an excellence barrier, but receiving the feedback brought it to my attention.
- By *applying theory in the dark,* I can assess other physical attributes that highlight a lack of self-discipline, which is the underlying reason why my diet is poor.

Just look at all the positives that can come from taking action on unrelated and negative feedback! You should also consider that our knowledge is necessarily limited. People often use the term "common sense", but I have yet to find any sense that is common. Everybody has gaps in their knowledge and differences in perspective, and you may find that the feedback you thought was negative actually removes your excellence barrier. If, on the other hand, you decided not to take action on negative feedback, you would have never come to this realization. Let us go through another fictional scenario that demonstrates this possibility.

Jake, entering professional development meeting: "Hey John, what is keeping me from growing my professional brand?"

John: "Do you want critical feedback?"

Jake: "Of course."

John: "If I am being transparent, you should probably stop wearing shorts to work. Although it is fine as far as the dress code goes, they are unprofessional."

Jake: "Thank you for the critical feedback. I have yet to receive feedback as actionable as this and it is truly appreciated."

John: "You are very welcome."

Now I don't personally feel John's feedback helps me in any meaningful way. I have always worn shorts in the summer, and I have made it this far in my career. That being said, John's feedback is actionable and isn't counter intuitive to my excellence barrier, so I decide to take action anyways. I stop wearing shorts and replace them with dress pants. Six months later, I apply for an open position which would be a promotion – and I have to interview with John's boss for this position.

John's boss: "Before we start the meeting, I do want to mention we appreciate your attire. Although this isn't a decision point for the position, it is nice to see you take pride in your professionalism."

The interview goes well, and I get the promotion! Now, in this example, of course the pants didn't get me the job. They were, however, a contributing factor! I took action on feedback I *thought* was negative, and it actually went a long way to removing my excellence barrier.

In all the examples up to this point, I have solicited feedback from my superior. This is often the default mode when it comes to soliciting feedback. However, it is just as important to solicit feedback from peers and subordinates, even though it may be uncomfortable.

Before we move on to the next chapter, it is important to note that all the examples in this chapter centered on removing *personal* barriers to excellence. It is important to solicit feedback when solving individual problems, but it is just as important to solicit feedback when solving team issues. If your team is experiencing an undesirable outcome, take the time to solicit feedback from the team before crafting an improvement vision. Ask why it happened, what we could have done differently, and ask for team recommendations. Teams are generally smarter than individuals and soliciting feedback will help the team behave as a team.

Chapter Five Recap

     Soliciting advice is one of the most effective ways to gain perspective. Additionally, it draws people in and creates comradery and teamwork. Soliciting feedback can be difficult because it requires the suppression of ego and is a vulnerable position to put yourself in. Reorient your mind to consider negative feedback as anything that you cannot take action on, and positive feedback as anything you can take action on. This will help take the sting out of feedback that you may perceive as a personal attack.

Chapter Exercises:

1. Take some time to talk to your significant other. Ask then what one thing you could do to make their life easier.

2. Schedule some time to one of your close friends that you do not work with. Ask them about an excellence barrier at work and how they might approach it.

3. Talk to a complete stranger and ask them for advice on a work problem you are experiencing. Their response might surprise you!

4. Continue to practice with people outside of work until you are confident that you possess the emotional maturity to flex this new habit in the workplace.

Chapter 6

Taking Smart Advice from Dumb People

Do you need the VP of communications to help you write an email? Do you need the CFO to weigh in on what pens to buy for the team? These examples seem ridiculous, but they highlight a habit that many individuals and organizations seem to exhibit. By default, we tend to look up as high as we can when seeking feedback. This likely stems from a need for affirmation, or a fear that solutions not generated from the top may not be accepted. Whatever the reason, this impulse can keep us from soliciting meaningful feedback. More often than not, it is our peers, subordinates, and total strangers that are holding the tools to removing our excellence barriers. You don't need a "higher" perspective, you just need a different one. That is why, when I refer to "dumb people", I do not intend to be diminutive; what I am really referring to is "people who you think are ignorant of your excellence barrier." Believe it or not, these people frequently have great feedback - sometimes more than a subject matter expert. I have an upsetting personal story about *taking advice from dumb people* I would like to provide as an example, along with a made-up scenario that further highlights why soliciting feedback from "dumb people" can be so helpful.

When I was 12 years old, I remember coming home from school one day and having nothing in the refrigerator. I heard my father get off the phone after speaking with his father, essentially begging him to pay the electricity bill for us this month. Apparently, my mother was given all of the money we had for the month and been told to pay the bill and get the groceries. She had a propensity to blow every penny she was ever given on lottery tickets, and this month was no different. As a result, we were broke and I was hungry. I approached my dad and asked him the following:

Jake: "Why do you keep handing her the money? How many times does this have to happen to us before we do something about it?

Dad: "Son, you can't blame a stupid animal for being stupid."

As a 12-year-old, I had no idea how to interpret this advice. First off, my father is not particularly intelligent, and – WOW – he was referring to his wife with that comment. I didn't know what to do with that response and wouldn't be able to apply it successfully for another 13 years.

Flash forward 13 years, and I am 25 years old, sulking at home with massive depression. I have just gotten a divorce, and I am curled up on the couch under 5 blankets for the second week in a row. I am reeling through all of my decisions in life, listlessly pondering what direction I could take going forward. My manic depression had led me down some particularly dark roads, but right there in the middle of it, I was struck with an incredible epiphany. I could clearly hear my father uttering the words, *"Son, you can't blame a stupid animal for being stupid."* I needed to apply that advice to *myself*. I was being stupid letting my emotions determine my self-worth, and although I had made some poor decisions in my marriage, I didn't need to blame myself. I was being what I was. In that moment, I learned to accept myself. Ironically, I ended up taking advice from my father, who at the time I considered to be quite dumb! I actually ended up internalizing his lesson in a myriad of ways, ultimately leading me to develop this principle and mindset change for seeking feedback. Literally anybody can offer feedback, and more often than not, it is good feedback. Even if it isn't good feedback, it doesn't hurt to ask. Let's look at a final fictional scenario where this is successfully applied.

Sven works as a chemist in a highly specialized, top-secret laboratory. He is running into a problem where several of his subordinates are often found off task, loitering around in common areas. Some time after work, Sven takes his family to an ice cream shop.

Cashier: "Thank you sir, that will be $9.50."

Sven, handing the cashier a ten-dollar bill: "Here you are."

Cashier: "Fifty cents is your change, is there anything else I can help you with today?"

Sven: "Yes sir, you can give me some advice with my employees. They seem to be off task quite a bit and I am not sure what to do about it."

Cashier: "Have you tried anything to incentivize productivity? Or even talked to the staff about your concerns?"

Sven: "Thank you for the answer, you have given me actionable feedback, sir!"

Cashier: "Anytime. Happy to help."

In the scenario above, what did we learn? We learned that anybody, from any walk of life, seniority, skillset, or education can provide meaningful feedback when it comes to removing an excellence barrier. Even if the cashier's response was "your employees are not my problem, good day", it wouldn't have hurt. Lean on strangers, spouses, subordinates, trainees, leaders, or even the internet to provide feedback. Feedback is a warm blanket in the cold world of excellence barriers. Wear it well.

Chapter Six Recap

Our egos are constantly tempted to think of others as less smart, intelligent, or enlightened than we are – and sometimes we are right. Nevertheless, developing the skill to solicit and use advice from all people is a cornerstone of your ability to work with others in the pursuit of excellence. Develop this skill by intentionally paying attention to advice that you consider beneath you.

Chapter Exercises:

1. Can you think of someone that keeps trying to give you advice that you ignore? Write their name down, and the advice they try to give you:

_____

_____

_____

_____

_____

2. Take a few minutes to think through this advice. How can it help you break down excellence barriers?

3. Why do you think this person is offering you this advice? Do you think that listening to them can strengthen your relationship?

Chapter 7

Finding Levers

Every human being on this earth has a lever or two. A "lever" is a straight-line motivator that when triggered, incites action. I personally like to imagine it as a pull string in a talking doll's back. Pull the string, and the doll talks. Humans are a bit more complicated than talking dolls, but we all have levers that incite action[3]. Some of these are obvious – if our child is in danger, for example, we rush to their aid. Others are more subtle – a desire to be the best or to avoid risk for example. There are all kinds of levers; for many people it is money or opportunity, while for others it is fun, inclusion, or even praise. Understanding this is critical to your personal improvement, because in many cases, both a barrier to excellence and a solution can be clear, but those who need to take action lack the necessary motivation to remove the excellence barrier. Understanding what motivates others is a key component to including others on the path to excellence. To help you understand levers, begin by understanding your own. Start by reviewing areas in your personal life where you are immediately interested in taking action. To help you recognize your own levers, let me share a few of my own.

- Writing – I first met a personal mentor in my life when he had written a beta copy of a book and solicited feedback. I provided feedback, and immediately realized that I wanted to write, and nothing was going to stop me.

---

[3] Cialdini, Robert. *Influence: The Psychology of Persuasion.* Harper Business, 2006.

- Continuous Improvement – Whenever I hear "we have always done this way" I am immediately triggered to look for a better way of doing things.

- Praise – I fall in the category of people that will go far above and beyond what is expected just for an "atta boy" or two.

- Money – Just like most people, money is important to me, and maximizing my compensation is a lever for me.

Knowing your own levers can be an effective tool in self-management. Now that I know my own levers, I can use them to manage myself whenever I seem to be getting in my own way. Let's draw up a few scenarios that highlight how this can be done.

I want to lose weight. I love sweet foods and finds excuses to eat. I spend $10 a day at the vending machine. This is an excellence barrier.

Now we have our "excellence barrier", and we have a really good solution without putting too much thought into it. Drop the fatty foods, eat more vegetables, exercise – the whole "healthy lifestyle" thing. That being said, just because I have a solution doesn't mean I am going to execute well. In fact, in this present moment, I am almost motivated to leave this excellence barrier up. So how exactly do we break that? All we really need to do is use my personal levers to motivate different behaviors.

- Writing – Perhaps I could keep a journal or blog to write about my lifestyle habits and goals. I might even start a social media account dedicated to my efforts.

- Continuous Improvement – I am enthusiastic about results, so perhaps I can create metrics demonstrating continuous improvement, such as BMI tracking, caloric intake, macros, and food choice scores.

- Praise – If I communicate my goals to my spouse, she can help me achieve my goal by praising me every time my metrics improve, or she witnesses a desired behavior or choice.

- Money – Since money is a lever for me, I can track the savings from not purchasing vending machine foods and celebrate the retained revenue.

It was relatively easy for me to use my levers to motivate a change in my behavior once I became aware of them. If you work with a high performing team, I suggest you let your team know your levers, and be mindful of them. This level of openness not only fosters teamwork, but also lets your team know that you are committed to helping them solve their problems, and how they can help you help them! This also allows you to be immediately motivated once you have a solution, fast tracking the removal of your team's barrier to excellence. Unfortunately, most people don't advertise their levers, or they have a disconnect between *what they think their levers should be versus what their levers actually are.* Just keep in mind that your true values and levers are revealed by your actions. Always.

Once you have practiced finding levers through self-examination, you are ready to find the levers of your team. There are two main approaches to discover a person's primary levers and having both skillsets is integral to both discovering levers and motivating your team toward common excellence goals.

Approach #1 – *Soliciting feedback with the "Start, Stop, Continue" methodology.*

This approach uses the "start, stop, continue" method to discover primary levers. To do this, we formally interview any member from our team and ask them three questions – what should we start doing, what should we stop doing, and what should we continue doing. Let's consider the following scenario:

Robert works as a manager in a high-volume post office. His job is to get all of the mail out by the end of the shift, ensuring the productivity and happiness of his employees. One of his duties is to conduct a weekly roundtable and drive projects around productivity and a positive work environment. He has struggled with the last several meetings to get any actionable feedback. This week, he decides to exercise one-on-one meetings with his team, deploying the start, stop, continue methodology.

Robert: "Hi Samuel. Today I wanted to bring you into a one-on-one to discuss some areas of improvement in the operation. If I could start by asking, what is something you would like to see the post office start doing?"

Samuel: "Well, I can't really think of anything. Maybe buy us lunch on Fridays?"

Robert: "Thank you. What is something we can stop doing?

Samuel: "Well, you could stop harassing us for the end of our break periods. Is a long break really a big deal?"

Robert: "Thank you. What is something you would like to see the post office continue to do?"

Samuel: "Hmmm. I really like the safety bonus. I would like to see that continue, and of course; get larger."

Did you notice how Robert did NOT give feedback to the employees' responses? The purpose of this exercise is not to justify why you aren't doing something, or why you won't stop. The purpose of this conversation is to understand what Samuels' primary levers are. If we are defensive or have an answer for everything, we cloud the issue and increase the likelihood that Samuel will be less forthcoming in the future. What did we learn about Samuel? Well Samuel has the following primary levers:

- Money – Samuel mentioned that he appreciated a performance-based bonus and would like to see it grow. Few people will argue that money is not a motivator, but keep in mind that this is usually the smallest lever at your disposal. It doesn't matter how much you pay people if you treat them poorly or if there is a toxic workplace culture. Often, the recognition that comes along with a bonus is more important than the money itself[4].

- Praise – When Samuel asked for lunch, he is actually asking for recognition and appreciation, rather than food.

- Autonomy – It might be easy to write off Samuel's comment about "not being harassed" for taking long breaks but recognize the motivation behind the words. Samuel is actually looking for autonomy, and chafes at the idea that someone else needs to manage his time for him.

Having debriefed Samuel, Robert approaches Brittany with the same strategy.

[4] Amabile, Teresa, and Kramer, Steven. *The Progress Principle: Using Small Wins to Ignite Joy, Engagement, and Creativity at Work.* Harvard Business Review Press, 2011.

Robert: "Hi Brittany. Today I wanted to bring you into a one on one to discuss some areas of improvement in the operation. If I could start by asking, what is something you would like to see the post office start doing?"

Brittany: "We could definitely start a suggestion box. I have loads of ideas about organizing the stock area."

Robert: "Thank you. What is something we can stop doing?

Brittany: "Well, if we could share the spotlight around in our meetings, I would like time to discuss areas of opportunity with the team. We don't like that you have all of the speaking time."

Robert: "Thank you. What is something you would like to see the post office continue to do?"

Brittany: "Hmmm. I really like the hours, PTO plan, and flexibility with my child. If I had to pick something, I really would like the shift rotation to continue as we have had it for the past months."

Robert now deduces Brittany's primary levers:

- Continuous improvement – Brittany mentioned use of a suggestion box. This indicates that she is interested in continuous improvement in the true sense of the word: team feedback resulting in removing excellence barriers.

- Team involvement – Brittany wants to speak in meetings; this indicates a penchant for leadership and desire for the team to be involved in recognizing and solving barriers to excellence.

- Work Life Balance – Brittany mentioned how she has some difficulty balancing her work responsibilities with her home life. Like many of us, work-life balance is an important, recurring problem.

- Leadership – Brittany's commentary on suggestion boxes and speaking up in meetings show you that she is motivated by leadership.

Robert now understands both Samuel and Brittany's primary levers. With this data, he can approach solving excellence barriers by appealing to their primary levers. Robert has a few excellence barriers of his own running the day to day of the post office and needs to deploy the correct strategy to overcome them.

Robert's first excellence barrier
There are two daily drops that need to go to the bank; one at break, and one at the end of the shift. Rob has been doing this for some time but needs to delegate to the team. These bank drops consume nearly two full hours and not only keep Robert from doing other, more value-added leadership tasks, but they also take him away from his site and team.

Robert decides to give the first drop to Samuel. Samuel is a fine employee that values autonomy. This drop can be made immediately after Samuel's break time, so it gives him the autonomy to self-regulate, while also kind of giving him a longer break. It is a win-win. Robert then gives the end of day drop to Brittany. By doing this, Robert gives Brittany the flexibility to make the drop a bit early and then go straight home if her home life requires it. Now imagine if Robert had not taken the time to learn about his employees. Robert might have ended up turning these opportunities into chores and creating resentment with his team!

Robert's second excellence barrier
Robert has too much work to do! In a day's time, he has twelve hour's-worth of work to fit in an eight hour shift. What can he do?

To start, Robert appoints Brittany the owner of the round table meeting. She is tasked with getting action items together and submitting them to make this a productive, fun work environment. This saves Robert time spent conducting meetings. Then, he bullet-points action items he must conduct on a daily basis, then breaks them down into what he feels comfortable delegating. Once he has this, he pulls Samuel into his office, reviews the list, and offers a pay increase to take on some of these duties.

Using the start, stop, continue methodology to solicit feedback allows you to understand your team and utilize their levers to remove barriers to excellence. It will also promote a higher level of work-life satisfaction in your team, as their duties are aligned with their motivators. There is another approach you can use with the start, stop, continue method that will also increase your understanding of team motivators. It is the same process, but rather than carefully structured, formal meetings, the method is applied during regular conversations through active listening.

Approach #2 – *Active listening with the "Start, Stop, Continue" Methodology.*

This is the same process; but it requires more intentionality. Essentially, during day-to-day conversations, listen for these same social cues, deriving your team's levers through open listening. This is a habit that you must develop, but it often gets closer to the truth than formal feedback. There is just something about regular, every-day conversations that helps people put their guard down. Let's assume Robert never solicited formal input with the start, stop, continue methodology, but is instead listening for it. Examine the following conversation.

Robert: "Okay guys. I am going out for lunch. See you in about an hour."

Samuel: "I like lunch."

Brittany: "Okay see you around. We should probably pitch in and all do lunch together sometime."

What did we learn about Samuel and Brittany from their responses? Let's start with Samuel. What did he mean by "I like lunch"? What did he *really* mean? While it is difficult to convey tone in a book, it is easy to imagine that he is implying more than just the fact that he enjoys food. He is communicating a desire for recognition, fellowship, and belonging. In much the same way, Brittany's response indicates that she values team unity, inclusion, and leadership. These are the same levers we learned while intentionally soliciting for them, but were uncovered in an organic way through Robert's intentional listening. It may take a few conversations of intentional listening, but in time, Robert will develop a well-rounded understanding of his team's motivations. It is integral we blend both methods into our strategy, so that we can understand how our team members are motivated.

Understanding your levers, and the levers of your teammates, is foundational to understanding more effective means of motivation to remove excellence barriers; use both formal meetings and active listening combined with the start, stop, continue methodology to understand these levers.

Chapter Seven Recap

Your ability to influence team members is related to understanding what motivates them. You can solicit feedback from your team members to find their personal levers – notice how this skill relies on developing previous skills in this book. You can utilize the "start, stop, continue" methodology to quickly uncover the levers of your team-mates.

Chapter Exercises:

1. Practice the "start, stop, continue" methodology with yourself in the mirror. Ask yourself what you should start, what you should stop, and what you should continue. Your answers may surprise you!

2. Find a practice partner, and practice using the "start, stop, continue" methodology in casual conversation.

3. Select a trusted individual at work to practice this methodology on. Tell them that you are practicing and ask them to provide feedback on how you did and how you made them feel.

Section Recap

Section two is about others – changing the way that you think about your interactions with other individuals. Each person is unique, and the skills presented in this section are designed to help you interact more effectively with the individuals you interact with and rely on daily to get things done and overcome barriers to excellence.

Soliciting Feedback

This habit serves as the bridge between your own vision of excellence and those around you whose buy-in you must have in order to be successful. Soliciting feedback is the habit of asking others for input in solving excellence barriers and is foundational to the remaining skills in this book.

Taking Smart Advice from Dumb People

This skill naturally builds upon the previous skill. While you might be willing to seek feedback from others, at a certain maturity level we all pick and choose who we listen to. Not only does this close us off from valuable feedback, it prevents us from learning a valuable skill. Learn to listen with humility and engage all people in your journey to excellence.

Finding Levers

Once you have developed the skill of soliciting feedback from – and listening to – all kinds of people, you are prepared to develop the skill of finding levers. Levers are straight-line motivators that move people to action. Knowing another person's levers allows you to cooperate on change projects and quickly gain their support in the removal of excellence barriers.

Section Three – Excellence in the Workplace

In section one we learned about four essential paradigm shifts that will impel you toward an excellence mindset. In section two we learned three tools that to help foster inclusion and understanding as you draw others into your excellence journey. The seven tools in these first two sections are primarily *relational*. They deal with how you relate to yourself and the world around you, and how you relate to others.

This final section deals with tools and methodologies that can be applied to your work environment. In this section we will examine seven tools to apply in your workspace to achieve excellence. This section is last for a reason. While the tools in this section are easier to understand and implement than those in the previous sections, it is important to develop self-knowledge and awareness, as well skill in dealing with others, prior to using your excellence tools in the workplace.

Consider these tools as similar to the wrenches and screwdrivers in a racing team's garage. Anyone should be able to use them, but until you understand the theory of racing, and until you know your driver's skills and preferences, attempting to use those tools in a race could result in disaster.

In similar fashion, practice the tools found in the first two sections of this book before using the tools in section three.

Chapter 8

Show Me Don't Tell Me

The father of just-in-time production, Taiichi Ohno, popularized the concept of a "Gemba Walk". What does Gemba mean exactly? It is Japanese for "the actual place". The whole idea behind this method is being to discuss excellence barriers at the precise point the barrier is being experienced. Not in a conference room, on the telephone, or *near* the area where the problem occurs. Gemba Walks address problems exactly where they are found. In similar fashion, *show me don't tell me* encourages you to go directly to where an excellence barrier is occurring and see it for yourself. Now let us create a scenario that drills into this principle and applies it successfully.

Jessica just started her new job as a manufacturing supervisor. She is in charge of managing 300 workers from 8am to 5pm and is in charge of checking out and returning equipment. The factory has had hooks for members of the team to place their hard hats on at the end of the day; however, leadership has generally been unsuccessful in getting the team to use the hooks. As a result, employees often show up to work and don't have a hard-hat to wear. This has resulted in significant costs to the company for equipment that should last for years. In Jessica's first few days, a meeting was held in the boss's office to discuss how they are going to get employees to return their hard-hats at the end of the day. Below is a conversation from that meeting.

Boss: "How can we get the team to return the hard hats to the hooks at the end of every shift?"

Larry: "We can't. We have tried everything. The team members are all worried their hat will be stolen by another member of the team, and don't want to show up to work only to be turned away. If they bring them home, they know they will have them and can actually work that day. But then they forget to bring them to work, or lose them, and we have to replace them."

Jessica: "Have we tried numbering the hats and assigning them?"

Larry: "We tried that, too many new faces in a work week and a signup sheet was more hassle than it is worth."

Jessica: "Have we tried disciplining the members of the team that have taken the hats home?"

Larry: "We tried that too, but too many people ended up losing their jobs or quitting and frankly, production needs the people; we can't afford to focus on this."

Jessica: "I understand, have we just tried being in that section at the end of shift, policing the hat hooks?"

Larry: "Of course, we are there every single day. It is just too much to handle. Too many people in too small of a space and everybody just wants to go home."

At this point Jessica could have 100 valid solutions to the problem, but they will all fall on deaf ears in this environment. Instead, Jessica applies *show me don't tell me* and instead says the following:

Jessica: "I understand Larry. Why don't we observe the hat station at the end of shift today, and brainstorm a solution together?"

In this scenario, Jessica knows she can develop an answer to the excellence barrier, but she just needs to understand what is really going on, and she needs Larry's buy-in as well. By ending the conversation in the boss's office and moving it to the location of the excellence barrier, she is in fact iterating towards excellence. Now we arrive at the end of the shift; let's see how this conversation continues.

A buzzer sounds, and with that sound comes 300 sweaty team members ready to hang their hats and go home.

Jessica: "Observation number one, almost everybody is already hanging their hats; I don't see the issue."

Larry: "Yeah well it's really the saw team that is bad about it."

Jessica: "Okay, can you tell me when that team is coming through the area, and their designated hat rack station?

Larry: "Well they don't have a designated hat rack station anymore, we took it down after they weren't using it."

Jessica: "Then how do we expect them to hang their hats?"

Larry: "I guess we don't, we all agreed on the shop floor it wasn't enough of a problem to deal with."

Jessica: "Okay, is this the saw team coming up?"

Larry: "Yes."

Jessica, approaching saw team: "Excuse me, team! I am Jessica, the new supervisor, and one of our excellence initiatives is hard hat management. If you could please all give me your hats, we will get you a special station to return and check them out from."

The team members begin handing over hats, and Jessica proceeds to set up the new hat-hook station. Jessica continues to observe its use with Larry for a few days, and the issue is largely resolved. Now let's take a look at what we learned from this real-life example.

What began as a large meeting in the boss's office had a simple solution. By utilizing *show me don't tell me*, we very rapidly removed an excellence barrier. Sometimes we can easily forget this is the easiest tool in our toolbox to use. If you can't remove an excellence barrier immediately, *show me don't me*. If you don't know why a barrier to excellence exists or what it truly is, *show me don't tell me*. Even if you think you know what a problem is or how to solve it, *show me don't tell me*.

Show me don't tell me is nothing more than having the discipline to take your team members to the place where the excellence barrier is happening and observing what is happening in real time and what you can do about it. This is the difference between *data* and *facts*[5]. In the preceding example, the team had financial data indicating that they were spending too much money on hard hats, but it wasn't until leadership practiced *show me don't tell me* that they were able to observe and understand the facts that led to those outcomes. Use *show me don't tell me* to quickly understand your barriers to excellence and you will not only achieve swift outcomes, you will also build team agreement and unity.

---

[5] In Lean management systems, emphasis is placed on *genchi genbutsu*, or "the actual place" where an issue occurs. Lean also emphasizes the difference between *data* – which is a number or metric indicating something is wrong, and *facts*, which comprise the true situation on the ground leading to those outcomes.

Chapter Eight Recap

"Show me, don't tell me" is a philosophy that values observation of a barrier to excellence above talking about a barrier to excellence. This is an important skill set to develop, because the true state of things is often lost in translation. Sitting around a conference room talking about negative outcomes is not the same as observing the process resulting in those negative outcomes. In Lean management philosophy, this is explained as the difference between *data* (bad outcomes, such as spending too much money on hard-hats) and *facts* (such as the reality that the saw team does not have a place to store their PPE). "Show me, don't tell me" is the habit of going to see the actual work before planning an excellence initiative.

Chapter Exercises:

1. Can you think of a time when you tried to solve a problem on the basis of a report or numbers without going to see the actual work? How did it turn out for you?

2. Take some time to think of a barrier to excellence in your work-place. Schedule some time to observe the process or processes that result in the barrier to excellence.

3. As you observe the process, take notes on what is really going on, and the activities or choices resulting in the barrier to excellence.

4. Do this several times to hone your skill, then take a coworker along and practice the exercise with them.

Chapter 9

Ascribing Figures to Qualitative Outcomes

Some things are easy to measure, while others may not appear so at first. Despite intuition, and everything school ever taught you, *everything* can be measured. This can be a difficult lesson to conceptualize and apply effectively, so I will provide three distinct scenarios. You see, anything can be effectively measured; it all depends on the approach. Let us say you work as a teacher, teaching 7th grade English. You have a traditional grading system for your students' performance; however, you want to go a step further. You want to *know how your lessons are affecting your students' speech*. While this may initially seem impossible to effectively measure, we can get close be considering the parts that add up to this desired outcome. This is a practical application of *breaking complex barriers into chunks* that we learned earlier. Since we find it prohibitively difficult to measure "how my lessons are affecting my students' speech", we instead decide to measure "things that are spoken incorrectly". This *is* able to be measured objectively, and *is* a contributing factor to the outcome we want to measure. Remember, if you have trouble measuring a positive outcome, you can always try to measure a negative outcome that *subtracts from* the outcome you are looking for. If these negative outcomes reach zero, you are probably very close to accomplishing your objective.

Once we have decided what to measure, we need to invent a grading scale. In this case, we decide that the class gets a default score of 100, and every time the teacher hears poor English grammar or enunciation, you will place a tally mark on the board. The teacher subtracts one point for each tally mark on the board. Now we have a score and everyone can see it. This allows us to easily take actions that improve this score over time, such as coaching students when we put a mark on the board, teaching lessons relevant to the behaviors we have been correcting, rewarding good grammar, and updating the class score weekly. We took a seemingly impossible task and created an incredibly simple method to measure it and track toward improvement. This is possible because in the pursuit of excellence we are not worried about absolute scores or being perfect. We are only concerned with getting *better*, and this kind of measurement system allows us to track and display directional improvement.

Now let's take this up a notch and measure something everybody thinks is impossible. Can we measure *love*?

Let's look at how we proceeded last time. We know we can't measure something as subjective and ephemeral as love, but we can flip this around in the same way, target our spouse, and say "let's measure things *they* love." You may not be able to measure love, but you can measure *behaviors*. And behaviors are certainly an important part of love.

Start by talking to your spouse or significant other – what does he or she love to do or love when you do? After some brief giggles at how funny the whole exercise is, you agree on the following list:

- Rub my feet
- Bring me snacks when you come home from work
- Take the trash out
- Clean the bathroom
- Kiss me

This is a clear cut list of measurable actions; now we just need a way to measure progress. One way we could do this would be to start with a 0 for the week, and we add a point for each action item taken. If your spouse loves some things more than others, you can even give the items different scores – surely a kiss scores more than taking the trash out! Measuring the score over time generates a run chart and helps you see your improvement. Take additional actions, iterate toward a score of 100, and ask for more bullet points as time moves forward. Slowly but surely you are developing an exceedingly good barometer for how much action you are taking that your spouse loves.

Consider a third situation that is subjective and nebulous. Let us pretend you are the proud new owner of a fast food restaurant. You make good profits, the store is generally clean, and the customers are reasonably happy. You however, being the over achiever that you are, want to measure how successful you are at entrepreneurship. This may seem like a tough idea to ascribe a metric to, but you guessed it; that is precisely what we are going to do. Just like in the first two examples, let us flip this phraseology to "things that look like success to me". Start by making a quick bullet point list of 4-5 things that look like success to you. My examples are the following:

- Profit Margin
- Cleanliness
- Customer Satisfaction
- Business Growth
- Employee satisfaction

Can you guess what we are going to do next? We are simply going to create a chart and measure our profit margin week over week. We are going to create a gradient scale of what cleanliness looks like, starting at 100 and taking off 10 points for each non-compliance we find. We are going to solicit customer feedback weekly on a scale of 1-10 and track week over week. We are going to trendline total sales week over week, and we are going to solicit employee feedback weekly on a scale of 1-10 and track week over week. As long as we take action against each of these metrics when they move in the wrong direction, we are treating towards excellence by our very own definitions.

I want to reiterate that your chosen metrics must be *actionable* to be *valuable*. It is not worth anybody's time to measure something and not take action when the measurements aren't above a goal line. You will never solve anything in life if you do not take action. The excellence barrier wouldn't exist if it would resolve itself with zero action. We need to be the catalysts of tearing it down and iterating towards excellence. *The speed at which we tear down excellence barriers is the gold standard.* Don't settle for mediocrity, complacency, or even perfection. Aim for better. Learning how to measure and iterate toward excellence is a prerequisite for taking action.

Chapter Nine Recap

It is difficult to intentionally improve what we are not measuring. Sometimes we struggle to measure things that are qualitative. Qualitative metrics can often be measured by correlating behaviors with desired outcomes and using a negative score to track directional improvement. Although absolute numbers cannot always be measured, all outcomes can be measured directionally with a little bit of patience and creativity.

Chapter Exercises:

1. Think of a metric in your work life that is not objective. What objective behaviors can you measure that might result in the positive outcomes you want?

2. How can you measure those behaviors?

3. Create a scoring system for those behaviors, and a graph to track your scores over time.

4. Use this scoring system and graph to practice tracking a qualitative outcome at work.

Chapter 10

Maintaining a Bias for Action

What separates a good leader from a poor one? What you will find is they almost all have the same answer. *The good one almost always does something the poor one doesn't.* Sometimes it is the other way around, with the good leader *not* doing something a poor leader is doing. In either case, it comes down to action. Let us peel that onion back a little bit.

Supervisor A is exceedingly good at managing his payroll. The time for his/her employees is always correct and verified before the deadline. Supervisor B always struggles to get this done timely, and there is almost always an error. Now before we dive into details, we can guess some things about the situation. We can guess that Supervisor A is probably doing something Supervisor B isn't. All things being equal, any difference in outcomes is generally attributable to actions. There isn't an internal human quality or magic spell that created superior outcomes, there is only "A took an action that B did not" (or vice versa). Now let us pretend that you are Supervisor B, and you have come up with the following reasons for why your outcomes are inferior to Supervisor A's outcomes. You may be surprised to find that they all have the same corrective action.

- Not given the same training as Supervisor A
- Has more work to do in other areas than Supervisor A
- Has more people and thus more payroll to manage than Supervisor A
- You often forget as you have other important deadlines when compared to Supervisor A

- You simply aren't as good as Supervisor A
- Supervisor A has been held accountable for not achieving this deliverable in the past and you have not
- There is a barrier to completion (such as system down time) that you must face that Supervisor A does not

Now let's break down each of these bullet points, and showcase how even though they are very different, they have the same solution.

- **Not given the same training as Supervisor A**

Maintaining a Bias for Action – Ask the training coordinator for the data you need to be successful. Work with Supervisor A and observe her process.

- **Has more work to do in other areas than Supervisor A**

Maintaining a Bias for Action – If you truly feel you are overworked, share your list of responsibilities with your boss and ask what duties can be shared or delegated. Otherwise this is just an excuse for not taking action.

- **You have more people and thus more payroll to manage than Supervisor A**

Maintaining a Bias for Action – Again, if you truly feel overworked, share your list of responsibilities with your boss and ask what duties can be shared or delegated. Otherwise this is just an excuse for not taking action.

- **You have other important deadlines when compared to Supervisor A**

Maintaining a Bias for Action – Take action around your forgetfulness. Write it down, add it to a calendar reminder. All you need to do right now is take action on your time management system.

- **You simply aren't as good as Supervisor A**

Maintaining a Bias for Action – Work with Supervisor A and observe the process. Practice with him until your process execution improves.

- **Supervisor A has been held accountable for not achieving this deliverable in the past and you have not**

Maintaining a Bias for Action – Do you need to wait for punishment to change your behavior? Take action on what motivates you to perform, and execute steps that make this a higher priority for you.

- **There is a barrier to completion (such as system down time) that you must face that Supervisor A does not**

Maintaining a Bias for Action – Showcase this to your leadership. Document the barrier and take whatever action you can to remove it.

In summary, do you see how we had a vast array of "reasons" for failure, but the methodology to correct was the same? All you need to do is *maintain a bias for action*. If you are ever unsure of which action to take, I have provided a handy tool at the end of this book which can coach you through which action to take or tool to use. As you get more and more familiar with a default response of *maintaining a bias for action*, you may begin to realize that many people do not have the same default response. As you are listening to social cues of leaders, peers, and direct reports, listen for action. If what they are saying as it relates to an excellence barrier isn't action oriented, there is a low probability for change to occur.

Another way to *maintain a bias for action* is to think to yourself, "What can I do right now?" when faced with a barrier to excellence. In the previous example, Supervisor B accepted *everything is your* fault, and used *breaking complex barriers into chunks* to help define what barriers needed to be overcome to get different outcomes. Some of these chunks needed a subject matter expert to resolve. But in every case, Supervisor B ended up with an action he could take right now. In the same way, when faced with an excellence barrier, don't be to hasty to turn its resolution into a project. Spend a few minutes thinking through the issue with the goal of arriving at what you can do right now. In this way you will *maintain a bias for action* and iterate toward excellence more quickly.

Chapter Ten Recap

Maintaining a bias for action is a centerpiece of both leadership behavior and culture building. This skill is based on the idea that change happens when people act, so acting on what you know right now is often superior than doing nothing or waiting for a perfect solution. This is closely related to *everything is your fault*, in that you have to take ownership before you can effectively take action. Remember, when in doubt, act.

Chapter Exercises:

1. Name an area of responsibility at work where you have failed to act. Why do you think that is?

2. Can you think of an action you can take right now to pursue excellence in that area of responsibility?

3. Does your team have a bias for action – what is the general culture?

Chapter 11

Discerning Value

Motion is not the same as progress. As you begin reorienting your paradigm around the pursuit of excellence, you may notice that your organization is focusing its resources on the "wrong" problem. Sometimes, energy is spent chasing phantom barriers. These are either barriers that do not actually exist, or that do not provide positive impact upon solving. At times, and especially when you are too far entrenched in a particular environment, you may find yourself focusing on *issue resolution* and not *value creation*. Thankfully, there is a tried and true method to avoid this trap. When dealing with an excellence barrier, ask yourself *"What value does solving this create?"* If you cannot answer that question, or if you cannot *clearly* articulate the value, you may be stuck on a phantom barrier. When this happens, just let it go, if possible. Of course, it may be more difficult than this if a senior leader in your organization is determined to solve a phantom barrier; however, it is your responsibility to try and guide the team in the right direction. This approach is likely a new muscle to flex, so it must be diligently practiced even when dealing with the most mundane opportunity area. Below is an example of this methodology in practice.

Rebecca works as a fisherwoman down at the docks.

Rebecca: "I currently use a 10-foot net. I cannot seem to keep up with all of the fish and miss out on opportunities. Many times, fish are spilling out of the sides."

- **Rebecca's small net prevents her from realizing opportunity**

What value does solving this create? – A bigger net nets more fish, which translates to more income for Rebecca. This is real value; proceed to secure a larger net.

Rebecca: "I would like a nicer boat. Mine is old and rusty".

- **Rebecca's old, rusty boat is unpleasant**

What value does solving this create? – Rebecca would be very happy in a new boat. Since you cannot articulate any real value effectively, you should not secure a new boat.

It is as simple as that, really. The hardest part is practicing this behavior until it becomes a habit. No matter how mundane the issue is, articulate the value of resolving it before taking action. If you cannot do so, move to the next opportunity. Your time and energy are incredibly valuable, and every second spent chasing a non-value-added improvement is a second wasted. Once more clearly defined barriers are removed, you can always come back to the problem. One way to think about this is "necessary" versus "nice to have". If you work in a package delivery service and have old trucks, you might consider an upgrade. However, if you are having trouble delivering packages on time, it is far more important to address that barrier to excellence first.

When an excellence barrier requires spending money, stray away from it if you cannot quantify the return on investment. This is an old "Lean" philosophy – how can you improve right now, with the resources you have? Chances are, you can solve your barrier to excellence with minimal capital expenditure. Some excellence barriers require capital expenditure, such as purchasing a milling machine. If you are considering purchasing a tool, and cannot quantify its ROI, do NOT purchase the tool. Do your homework first, and have a plan to *actually realize* the proposed ROI once you develop it.

There is merit, however, to considering "potential ROI". In fact, this is a frequently overlooked type of ROI. You may not "know" a quantifiable ROI, but you can still articulate potential value. Consider if you wanted to purchase professional headshots. There is simply no way to calculate real value or ROI on professional headshots, but you can clearly articulate "this will increase my professional presence, which has the potential to bring value to me". This type of unknown is okay, as long as you can articulate what excellence barrier you are trying to overcome, and what potential value it may bring.

In conclusion, develop the mindset of always articulating the value you will realize prior to expending time or effort on an excellence barrier. This can end up saving you and the team quite a bit of time and resources.

Chapter Eleven Recap

Before you can be truly effective at removing barriers to excellence, you will need to develop the skill of discerning value. Discerning value is the habit of assessing what value will be created (or destroyed) by the actions you plan to take. Discerning value will help you avoid wasting your company's resources and your team's time.

Chapter Exercises:

1. List all of the action prerogatives that your boss has given you. Define what value may or may not result from solving those issues. What percent can you ascribe a real dollar value to?

Chapter 12

When it is okay to Steal

Sam Walton, the founder of Walmart, was famous for telling people that he never had an original idea in his life. He recognized the value of "stealing" good ideas. You see, most of the barriers you will experience in life have already been experienced by somebody else. In most cases, they have been resolved successfully, many different times, and are just hanging from the world's lowest tree branch waiting to be plucked. While these solutions may not be *perfect*, they are *proven*, and are usually good enough to move the ball forward with minimal effort. There are only two limiting factors to applying this tool, and those are...

1. Actual theft
2. The ego barrier

When I talk about it being "ok to steal" I am talking about using other people's ideas to solve your own problems. Obviously we are not talking about actual theft of intellectual property. That would be wrong. But we have this amazing new tool called "the internet" where people post quite a bit of free content. This is a treasure trove of solutions that you can access for free.

When it comes to solving excellence barriers, there are literally thousands of books, articles, and videos designed to help you succeed. Use them! With the advent of the internet, many companies are even offering free software tools and templates immediately available for download.

Here are three example scenarios where "stealing" a solution is perfectly ok.

- **Jairo is tasked with creating a project plan for an upcoming business acquisition.**

When it is okay to Steal – Jairo does a quick internet search and finds a free template for his project plan. He uses it to great success and removes his biggest barrier – knowing what format a business plan should adhere to.

- **Rodney is tasked with creating a flyer for an upcoming office party.**

When it is okay to Steal – Rodney discovers that his company's print vendor has free design services. Rodney uses this service to design a killer promotional bill for the upcoming office party.

- **Mark is tasked with organizing a tool area in the warehouse.**

When it is okay to Steal – Mark recently toured a different warehouse in a different industry, but really liked the way the tool area was organized. Mark emulates this setup.

As the scenarios showcase, "stealing" ideas can provide an immediate improvement while reducing the amount of effort you have to expend in order to get results. You would be very surprised how many excellence barriers can be removed with a simple internet search. Always ask yourself when a barrier is represented "Is a viable solution already out there and available?" This may seem like common sense, but I am always surprised by how many people struggle to come up with a solution without first researching what others have done about it.

The ego barrier is another risk when using this tool When "stealing" a solution, you may very well be tempted to examine the data and say "that doesn't work!" It is human nature to disagree, and it is often pride that inhibits us from imagining that another person's solution is superior to our own – even if we don't have our "own" solution yet! This can be difficult to push past when reviewing ideas from a book or the internet. You may find yourself saying "that is just rhetoric" or "that is a good idea, but can't actually be applied". Anywhere you find yourself thinking this way, immediately ask yourself "Is my ego getting in the way?" It can prove difficult to police our own biases, but having the self-awareness to recognize when your own ego is getting in the way is incredibly helpful. We are imperfect creatures and subject to a wide range of influencing factors. When you find yourself in this mindset, try out the solution anyway. There is nothing more important than removing your excellence barrier – not your pride, your ego, or your personal biases. Take the solution proposed and apply it objectively.

Chapter Twelve Recap

You don't have to have all the answers or develop solutions from scratch. Before your ego forces you to be excessively creative and save the world with the might of your wit, look for an existing solution. Using existing solutions allows you to secure a "good enough" solution and free up resources to address the next excellence barrier.

Chapter Exercises:

1. List five areas in your work life or home life that need improvement.

   _____

   _____

   _____

   _____

   _____

2. Use the internet to research each area and find out if there is a solution you can apply right now.

Chapter 13

Process Mindset

In both personal and professional life, controlling your reaction to an issue/excellence barrier is more important than the barrier itself. If you constantly change *how you react* to a failure, you may actually be building in an additional propensity for failure. This makes sense, because, ultimately, barriers to excellence are removed through teamwork, and inconsistent responses to problems will result in team confusion. People will be so busy trying to please an inconsistent boss or coworker, that they may end up whipping back and forth between different types of problem solving, never giving a fix a chance to work, and never learning any consistent problem-solving methods through repetition. This type of confusion can be avoided by intentionally adopting a process-mindset. A process mindset looks at undesirable outcomes as the results of a process, rather than as the result of "employees not doing it right." This focus not only promotes consistent outcomes, it fosters an environment of judgment-free improvement opportunity.

Consider the following scenario: Lesley works as a supervisor in a manufacturing facility. Part of her job entails confirming the separation of cardboard and plastic discard. Leslie walks into work this morning and has an email in her inbox from her recycling provider, notifying her that the discard they collected was not properly separated.

Lesley, walking out into the shop floor: "What is the darned problem with getting this recycling thing right team? This is ridiculous!"

Note that Leslie's reaction didn't solve or alleviate the issue. Three days later, there is another email in her inbox, citing the same issue.

Lesley, walking out into the shop floor: "ALRIGHT, EVERYBODY GATHER UP FOR A MEETING."

Leslie proceeds to plead with the team to do better at discard separation. Note that this reaction didn't solve or alleviate the issue either. Also, the reaction is different. In the first example, Leslie complained in a general way to her team, while in the second, she held a more organized meeting asking for help. In both cases, however, Leslie didn't use any of the problem-solving tools we have looked at: *everything is your fault*, *PDCA*, or *applying theory in the dark*, for example. A month later, there is another email in Leslie's inbox, citing the same issue.

Lesley, stomping out onto the shop floor: "I am writing this entire team up! How can we not get this right???"

Note the issue is still not resolved. Now what is Lesley doing wrong exactly? When we read stories like this it is easy to tell that something is wrong, but we don't always take the time to consider *why* we think that. So what can Leslie improve? Well, first and foremost, Leslie isn't controlling her reaction to an excellence barrier. She is just being led by her emotions, resulting in knee-jerk reactions. Not only is this bad for business, it is bad for morale, and bad for problem solving. Secondly, Leslie is focused on *behaviors*, rather than *process*. By changing her approach, Leslie can more quickly recognize actual barriers to excellence, and remove them more quickly.

Let's see what happens when Leslie utilizes a process mindset.

Lesley, walking out into the shop floor: "We have a non-compliance today, team. I have brought copies of the process for review".

There are two keys to Leslie's approach. The first is that she focuses on the process and process compliance rather than on team members or their behaviors. This is important, because the key to consistent outcomes is having a single method of execution – this is called a process or procedure[6]. A clear, concise set of process instructions is the focal point of compliance. Of course, the primary way you can get humans to consistently follow a process is to have it written down, as a written procedure is less open to individual interpretation and can be referenced at will by the operator. The second key to Leslie's approach is her choice to use intentionally neutral language like "non-compliance" rather than emotionally invested words like "not getting it right". This is important, because by de-personalizing the situation, Leslie is much more likely to avoid the stubbornness that comes from people who feel judged. If your approach to problems makes people feel judged, they are likely to spend time justifying themselves, rather than solving the problem. They are also more likely to cover up problems – no one likes to feel judged!

While reviewing the process, the team uncovers some barriers to excellence. The first is that one of their highly used items has plastic affixed to the cardboard, and the employees do not have a tool to effectively remove it. The second is there are no visual indicators distinguishing the cardboard receptacle from the plastic receptacle. As a result of these two barriers, cardboard is often discarded with plastic still attached, and new employees often put discard in the wrong receptacle. Having observed these

---

[6] Technically, a process is a series of steps to convert inputs to outputs, while a procedure is the approved method for executing those steps. In the context of a local operation, this distinction is often meaningless, so we will use the terms interchangeably in this book.

barriers, Leslie secures tools for her team to separate the plastic from the cardboard, and also places clear signage over the receptacles distinguishing the cardboard from the plastic.

Compliance

Beginning with a process mindset allows you to effectively uncover barriers to excellence and create a continuous improvement culture, but in order for this to work, your team needs to actually follow the process. When examining any process failure, you should always consider three possible scenarios: First, is there a process in place? If there isn't a process in place, you can't expect consistent execution. Second, is there a process in place, but it failed? If the answer is "yes", then you should improve the process, as Leslie did above. However, there is a third question: is there a good process in place, and it just wasn't followed? If this is true, then the first thing you should examine is whether you have a solid training program in place and if your employee has been provided the knowledge and skills to perform their job successfully. In order to get the outcomes you want, process compliance must be clearly and consistently articulated to the team.

Accountability

Now comes the hard part - process focus and process compliance only work if they are held in conjunction with process accountability. The behavior that is required for a process to be a success or failure must directly be incentivized *and* de-incentivized. This is why companies have formal processes for documented accountability. It isn't enough to document and train to a process; the responsible employees must be held accountable through rewards and consequences. This should be the *last* step in your process paradigm, once you conclude that the process is sufficiently robust and that your team has sufficient training.

However, the time will come when you need to hold an employee accountable through fair and documented coaching. By utilizing a process mindset, you can put your team at ease that you have done everything you are responsible for to improve team success. You will also give yourself the confidence to perform your coaching knowing you took a fair approach. Writing people up is never fun, but fair and consistent accountability is necessary for excellence. Don't shirk this duty.

It is said that most human beings on this earth never evolve past an "action/reaction" way of thinking. By placing focus on disciplining *your* reaction to problems, you can transcend this binary way of thinking. It isn't easy, and it isn't fast, which is why it is called discipline. What if Lesley has a problem in her personal life? For example, what if Leslie has an ill-tempered dog at home, or a car that always breaks down. You may be tempted to think "these things are totally unrelated to work performance"; however, if Leslie disciplines her reactions to *these* barriers effectively, she is practicing reaction discipline that will quickly affect her work experience as well. By practicing consistency in response to excellence barriers, we are training ourselves for quicker and more effective execution across disciplines. The process mindset will empower her to control her response to outcomes failures and effectively drive change.

Reading through Lesley's journey, there is one other mission critical tool to resolving excellence barriers, which is especially powerful when excellence barriers are behavior based. Think of it this way - can you get a complete stranger to immediately hand you the results you want?

Chapter Thirteen Recap

Process mindset is the discipline of thinking of business outcomes as the natural result of a series of steps to convert inputs to outputs. There are two main components of process mindset: compliance and accountability. The team must be *compliant* with process requirements, and there must be *accountability* for behaviors that influence the process (but not necessarily for process outcomes).

Chapter Exercises:

1. List one metric that is important to your boss. Now write out all the steps that result in that metric, going back to when goods or data first enter your work area.

2. Now expand the previous exercise to stretch back to the entire building where you work.

3. What behaviors seem most important for the process to result in the outcomes you want?

Chapter 14

Making it Visual

You should always do everything in your power to make a process as similar to landscaping as possible. When your lawn doesn't look good, you immediately know it. And since lawncare is relatively simple, you probably also know what to do just by looking at your lawn. Does it look shaggy? Time for a mow. Is it looking a bit brown? Better water it. A landscape is a great visual indicator of how your lawn is doing and what actions you might need to take to get the outcomes you want.

Imagine if your car didn't come with a gas gauge. Yes, you could create a manual process to track your gasoline usage, but how much more often as a society would we have people stranded on the side of the road because they ran out of gas? You could always argue, "Well, we have gas gauges, but people still run out of gas, so it doesn't work." But that response misses the entire point of *making it visual.* The purpose behind *making it visual* isn't to fix anything, it is only to make current process outcomes clear. *Making it visual* allows you to quickly determine when there are barriers to success and can often point you in the right direction for correction. Consider the following example:

A local burger joint has an issue with special requests. Too often burgers come out with the wrong toppings, and the restaurant does not have a Point Of Sale system[7]. Let us brainstorm a few ways we could bring visual management to this excellence barrier.

- The restaurant could print the receipt, then give that receipt to the kitchen.
- The restaurant could mount a TV in the kitchen connected to a computer at the order counter. The clerk could write special instructions in a simple word processing program and have it display in the kitchen.
- The owners could make special request cards and leave the cards at the start of the service line, encouraging customers to fill out. These could be passed back to the kitchen.

All of these proposed solutions utilize the same principle. They use visual management to improve process compliance. None of these three solutions are perfect. Of course burgers will still come out wrong, but the purpose of *making it visual* isn't to *eliminate* the problem, it is to improve compliance. If you were to measure it, you might find that there is a 10% accuracy deficiency in special orders; *making it visual* might bring this down to 1%. It is human nature to look at everything as 100 or 0, "it is or it isn't", but that perspective is directly counter to removing excellence barriers. Always remember that if you cannot remove a barrier completely, you can still almost certainly minimize it. Let's look at another example:

Jerome is always late for work. He is looking for his keys every single day and it always gets him out of the door 5 minutes late. Jerome decides to address his challenge by *making it visual*. He comes up with three alternatives.

---

[7] A Point Of Sale system, or POS, is a digital platform for managing customer consumption and reorder of goods. In the quick-serve restaurant industry, a POS usually defines exactly how the customer configures their order, which is why on the drive-through screen you will often see your order as something like " 1 fantastic burger, + relish, - onions".

- Jerome will get a key hook and place it by the front door. Jerome will start using this visual tool to track where he places his keys.
- Jerome will place his keys with other critical items for his day such as his wallet, phone, or Laptop
- Jerome will stick a giant shiny trinket to the key ring so the keys stand out regardless of where he leaves them, at home or work.

Any of these items decrease the probability that Jerome will lose his keys, but none absolutely prevent him from ever misplacing his keys. Imagine, however, if every process you needed in order to be successful had *making it visual* built in. How much easy would your life be? How often would you be successful?

Chapter Fourteen Recap

Making it visual is intentional. You must determine to make the outcome of every process clear just by looking. Instead of relying on people to remember, think, or choose to "do the right thing", make what you want visually obvious to everyone.

Chapter Exercises:

1. Think of one process outcome that is important to you and the team. What one thing can you do right now to make it visual?

2. Now go do that one thing.

Section Recap

Section three builds on the previous two sections by extrapolating the internal and interpersonal lessons of sections one and two to encompass the physical working environment. Although the skills in this section are much easier to execute, it is important to build your personal and interpersonal mindset prior to attempting these habits.

Show Me Don't Tell Me

This section is about using physical space to understand your business outcomes. When you have a barrier to excellence, go the place where the work is done and watch the process in action prior to coming up with a solution. This will help you avoid jumping to conclusions.

Ascribing Figures to Qualitative Outcomes

Everything can be measured. If the thing that will make you successful is qualitative, find an objective behaviour to measure that will positively influence the outcome you are looking for. Create a scoring system and begin tracking your score. For example, if you track every piece of trash you pick up off the floor, a decreasing number *probably* means your work area is getting cleaner. This is close enough for the pursuit of excellence.

Maintaining a Bias for Action

When faced with a barrier to excellence, always ask yourself what you can do about it *right now*. This mindset is a critical part of your success; knowing all the theory in the world is not going to help you overcome barriers to excellence.

Discerning Value

Before spending resources to fix a problem, ask yourself what value you will gain by solving it. If you can't clearly articulate the value, skip the problem if possible.

When it is Ok to Steal

Tell your ego to shut up. You aren't special, and someone else already solved your problem probably better than you could. Use existing tools to implement "good enough" solutions that allow you to move quickly to the next barrier to excellence.

Process Mindset

Always consider your outcomes as the result of a series of steps to convert inputs to outputs. For your process to be *consistent*, you must have compliance and accountability. When you get outcomes you don't want, look at the process before blaming a person.

Making it Visual

Do everything you can to make the process and its outcomes visual.

Conclusion

If you have survived this far, you have successfully imbibed all of the information I have to share. You now possess the basic outline of how to solve ANY barrier. In the beginning of this book, I asked the question "What is the gold standard? What does excellence look like?" Well, I'd like to propose an answer.

The speed at which barriers to excellence are removed is the measure of excellence. Speedy recognition and resolution of barriers is the gold standard.

To expand this definition a little further, imagine any successful individual or company. It doesn't matter what field of expertise or avenue in life they experienced success, what matters is they focused solely on overcoming the barriers between themselves and excellence. That is why they are successful. Hypothetically, imagine you have your eyes set on a goal, and you have the tools and capacity to overcome anything and everything that gets in the way inside of 5 minutes. How long before you reach the goal? How long before you are successful? Well ladies and gentlemen, this book is that tool. Push past the gap between theory and application and use the tools in this book to knock down your own excellence barriers.

The Excellence Toolbox

Before applying *the excellence toolbox*, you will need to assess your own excellence barrier solving skills objectively. It is difficult to assess one's own behavior, but vital to utilizing *the excellence toolbox* effectively. Most people, when being brutally honest, fall into one of the three following categories - choose the one that best describes you before we continue:

- I am objectively bad at recognizing and eliminating excellence barriers
- I am really good at recognizing excellence barriers, but struggle to eliminate them at times
- I am a master of issue resolution and excellence barrier removal and am reading this book simply to entertain new ideas.

If the first bullet point describes you best, you must "throw out" all of your previous approaches to solving barriers. You must objectively use *the excellence toolbox* to a "T" and work to discipline your behaviors whenever you find yourself straying back to your old habits.

If the second bullet point describes you best, your prescription is the same. Having the ability to recognize barriers to excellence but lacking the skill to overcome them has the same practical outcome as the first category. You may be tempted to say, "I know the right answer and how to do it, but I just don't sometimes." To be fully transparent, that is your ego getting in the way of acknowledging that you don't have resolution skills. Now is not the time for self-pity or self-loathing; every human on earth has cognitive blind spots. What is important is that you recognize your opportunity for improvement and use *the excellence toolbox* to take you where you need to go. You, too, must follow *the excellence toolbox* to a "T" and work to discipline your responses in life to excellence barriers.

Finally, if the third bullet point describes you best, then I hope you had an enjoyable experience reading this book, and it gave you something to think about. Print out *the excellence toolbox* and hang it somewhere; you never know when it may assist in your personal journey to finding excellence in execution.

The Excellence Toolbox

This tool is designed to help you address your excellence barrier in a rational way by using and testing each tool in this book. Write your problem statement on the "Excellence Barrier" field. Put a checkmark in the "Conducted" column each time you use a method to try and solve your excellence barrier. When you find one that resolves your excellence barrier, put a check mark in the "Resolved" column. If you are feeling worried that you lack the ability to overcome excellence barriers, keep all of your work sheets for your first few barriers. You will begin to notice a trend in which of these methods produce the most results for you. This will build your confidence and also point you in a potentially successful direction in the future.

Excellence Barrier:		
Ways to Find Excellence	**Conducted**	**Resolved**
Everything is your fault		
PDCA then PDCA then PDCA		
Breaking complex excellence barriers into solvable chunks		
Applying Theory in the Dark		
Show Me Don't Tell Me		
Soliciting Feedback		
Taking smart advice from dumb people		
Ascribing figures to qualitative outcomes		
Maintaining a Bias for Action		
Finding your lever, and the lever of others		
Discerning value		
When it is okay to Steal		
Process Compliance, Process Accountability, and Process Fix		
Making it Visual		

Here is an example of how I used *the excellence toolbox* to overcome an excellence barrier in my own life:

Excellence Barrier: Jake wants to be an author, and has no firm direction		
Ways to Find Excellence	**Conducted**	**Resolved**
Everything is your fault	√	
PDCA then PDCA then PDCA	√	
Breaking complex excellence barriers into solvable chunks	√	
Applying Theory in the Dark		
Show Me Don't Tell Me	√	
Soliciting Feedback	√	
Taking smart advice from dumb people		
Ascribing figures to qualitative outcomes	√	
Maintaining a Bias for Action	√	
Finding your lever, and the lever of others		
Discerning value		
When it is okay to Steal	√	
Process Compliance, Process Accountability, and Process Fix		
Making it Visual	√	√

In this example, I always wanted to write something valuable. This has been on my mind for a few years now, but for one reason or another, I never saw to its completion. Here is how I applied the toolbox:

Everything is your fault – I began by taking ownership of seeing a project through to completion. It was nobody's fault but mine that I had not yet written a book.

PDCA then PDCA then PDCA – I made a plan to write this book by bullet pointing 30 actionable methods of resolving excellence barriers, and curated the list by practicing in real life. I then had to "do" by writing, "check" by reviewing the content, and "adjust" the text based on the results of the check.

Breaking complex excellence barriers into solvable chunks – Once I had an end goal of creating a book about overcoming barriers to excellence, I wrote several headers on what this might look like, and proceeded to explain each individual method. I broke all the headers down to their simplest form, then I conducted research and made an informed decision on which methods to include in the finished book. I used real-world testing and leveraged subject matter experts to help solve each chunk of the book.

Show Me Don't Tell me – I had two author colleagues of mine send me a beta copy of their own books to examine. This gave me an idea of what my finished product should look like.

Soliciting Feedback – I asked for feedback from one author colleague, one peer at work, my spouse, and one total stranger.

Ascribing figures to qualitative outcomes – I created a metric for tracking the completion of this project, then tracked my progress daily.

Maintaining a Bias for Action – I set a daily goal of words to write and held myself accountable to hit this target daily.

When it is okay to Steal – I "stole" the font and margins from a colleague of mine, and the word count along with a few styling cues from another. I stole the style and marketing from internet articles cataloguing what topics and content are being read and selling.

Making it Visual – I purchased a whiteboard and put it right by the television in my living room. I used this whiteboard to track the metrics I had developed. Once I was updating daily, and seeing the progress line, I had all of the tools in place to successfully resolve and complete this book!

Have an excellence barrier you want to talk about?

www.linkedin.com/in/JakeHarrellChasingExcellence

Made in the USA
Middletown, DE
09 January 2022

58242996R00064